W9-AKB-005

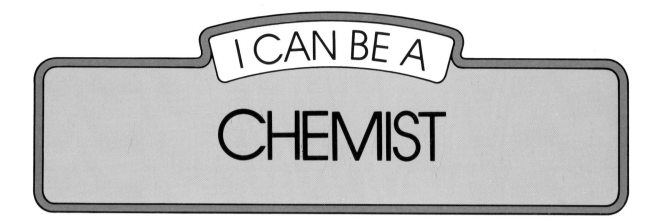

I CAN BE A

CHEMIST

By Paul P. Sipiera

868589

JUN 1 8 1993

ℙ CHILDRENS PRESS®
CHICAGO

CHILDRENS DEPARTMENT
BRADLEY LIBRARY

Library of Congress Cataloging-in-Publication Data

Sipiera, Paul, P.
  I can be a chemist / by Paul Sipiera.
    p.   cm.
  Summary: Describes the different kinds of work done
by chemists and the necessary training for entering the
field.
  ISBN 0-516-01965-1
  1. Chemistry—Vocational guidance—Juvenile
literature. [1. Chemistry—Vocational guidance.
2. Occupations. 3. Vocational guidance.] I. Title.
QD39.5.S57 1992
540'.23—dc20   92-5807
                                            CIP
                                            AC

Copyright © 1992 by Childrens Press®, Inc.
All rights reserved. Published simultaneously in Canada.
Printed in the United States of America.
1 2 3 4 5 6 7 8 9 10 R 00 99 98 97 96 95 94 93 92

Dedication: To the memory of James
            M. DuPont, a good friend
            and collector of
            meteorites.

PICTURE DICTIONARY

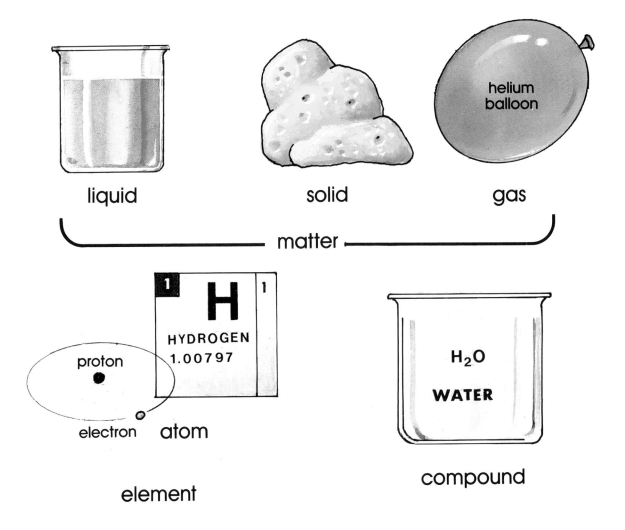

liquid   solid   gas

matter

element

compound

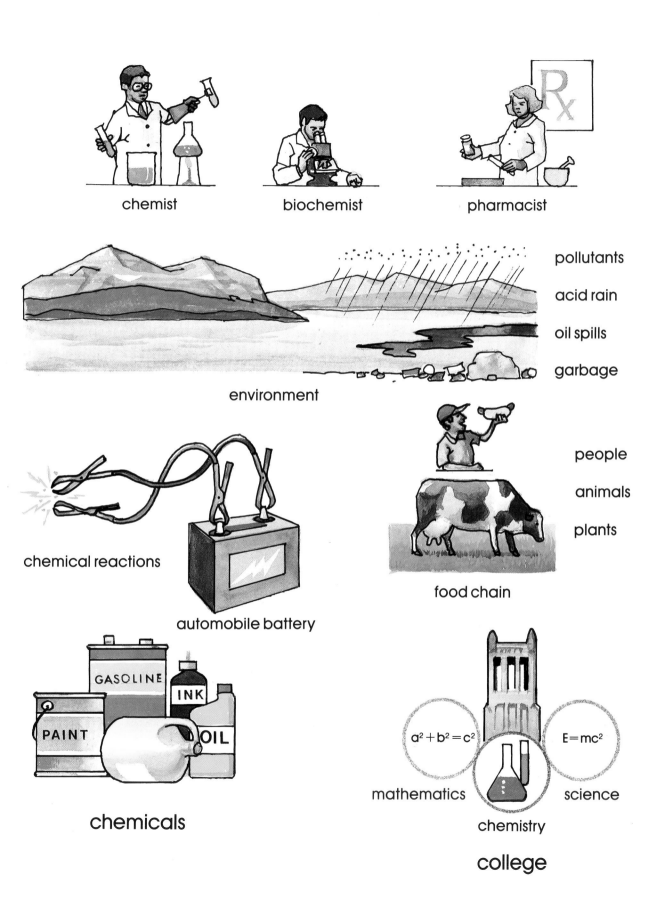

chemist

biochemist

pharmacist

environment

pollutants

acid rain

oil spills

garbage

chemical reactions

automobile battery

people

animals

plants

food chain

GASOLINE

INK

PAINT

OIL

chemicals

$a^2 + b^2 = c^2$

mathematics

$E = mc^2$

science

chemistry

college

Many different animals (above and left) live on the Earth. Over two-thirds of the Earth's surface is covered by water (below). The solid parts of the Earth are made up of many different rocks and minerals (below left).

The world we live in is made of rocks and soil, air and clouds, water, and all kinds of plants and animals. These things look different, but they are all made of the same material—matter.

Everything you see is made of matter. Matter can be a gas, a liquid, or a solid. Scientists who study matter are called chemists.

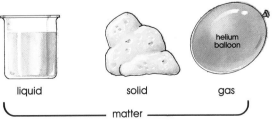

liquid   solid   gas

matter

Students experiment with heat to see how it changes a chemical reaction.

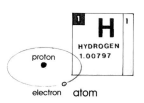

element

The smallest piece of matter is the atom. Chemists have learned that all matter found in nature is made from 92 different elements. Only one kind of atom is found in each element.

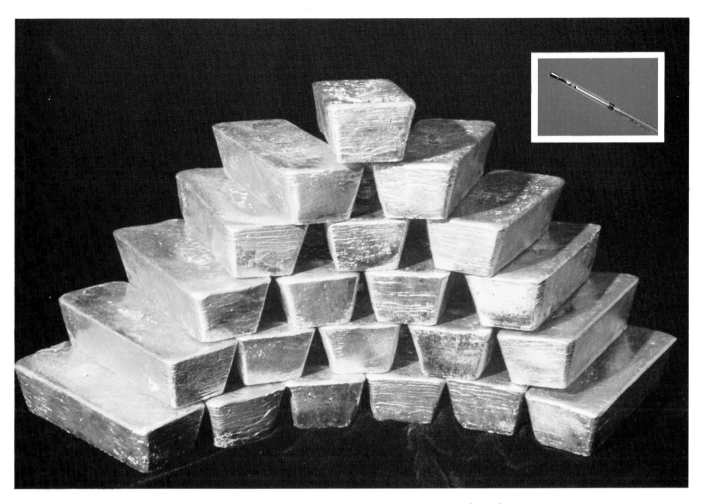

Gold is a very valuable element. A thermometer (inset) uses the element mercury to measure temperature changes.

Hydrogen, mercury, and gold are elements. Hydrogen is a gas, mercury is a liquid, and gold is a solid.

Calcium is an element that plays an important part in bone growth.

All living things are combinations of different elements. There is calcium in your bones and iron in your blood. Our bodies need certain elements to keep us healthy.

All living things need
water. Water is not an
element. It is a

compound

compound made of two
elements—hydrogen and
oxygen.

Biochemists give doctors important information that may help cure diseases.

chemist

biochemist

Chemists study the makeup of things. Some chemists study living things and are called biochemists. They help doctors. They examine blood and tissue samples. This helps the doctor find out what is making someone sick.

A pharmacist prepares drugs that help
people stay healthy.

Pharmacists know
chemistry. They know how
drugs work. They make
sure people get the right
drugs.

pharmacist

A rain forest is a very special environment.
It needs to be protected from
harmful chemicals.

Some chemists examine
our air or test our water.
They look for pollutants—
things that harm our
environment.

Pollutants like acid rain damage our lakes and forests. It is up to chemists to help find ways to solve pollution problems.

Acid rain can damage marble statues (top left) and spruce and pine trees (bottom left). In fact, acid rain can destroy a whole forest (above right).

pollutants

acid rain

oil spills

garbage

environment

Garbage and other waste products (left) can pollute our water supply. Polluted water kills valuable plants and animals. Then, less desirable plants and animals (right) may take their place.

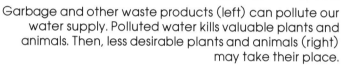

Garbage can be a pollutant. Chemists study garbage to learn how it decays. Certain kinds of waste can put harmful chemicals into our air and water supplies. This pollutes our environment.

Chemical wastes can make the environment unsuitable for life. Polluted areas must be closed to protect people from harmful chemicals.

Plants that we eat may take up these chemicals from the air or soil. Animals that we raise for food sometimes eat polluted food or drink polluted water. Most of

Good farmers take care of their land. They do not pollute water or soil.

people

animals

plants

food chain

the time we don't even
know it has happened.
But when chemical poison
gets into the food chain,
people, animals, and
even plants can get sick

Garbage dumped in landfills can pollute our water
supply if it is not properly controlled.

and may even die. A
chemist is needed to find
the source of the
pollution and then to
help clean it up.

Oil spills are very harmful to the environment. Chemists help find ways to clean up oil slicks. They also make cleaners that remove oil from birds and other animals safely.

Not all chemists work with living things. Some chemists work with metals. They help develop new materials. For example, by combining different elements with

Using cleaners made by chemists, workers wash oil off wild animals affected by oil spills (above). Oil spills (below) can damage the environment for many years to come. They must be cleaned up as soon as possible.

Iron is an important element that has many uses.

iron, a new, much harder
steel can be made.

We depend on
chemistry every day.
Automobile batteries
make electricity because

Refineries (above) make many things from oil. A chemist (right) uses different kinds of glassware to perform experiments.

of a chemical reaction between an acid and a metal. Gasoline and heating oil are produced by chemically refining crude oil.

chemical reactions

automobile battery

Different colors of paint are made by using different elements and compounds.

chemicals

Paints and inks are made from chemicals. Different elements give different colors. Chemists know how to make just the right shades of color.

Plastic is used for toys and containers because it can easily be shaped. However, dealing with plastic waste (top left) has become an important environmental problem.

Plastic was invented by chemists. It is now used in just about everything—from soda bottles to furniture.

When plastic is thrown away (left), it does not go away. It stays around for a long time. Carelessly discarded rings from canned drinks can kill wildlife (above).

Plastic is made to last a long time. It does not easily decay. Today chemists are making new plastics that decay quickly. This will help solve one environmental problem.

Chemicals added to our food can make it taste and smell better.

Chemists work in the food industry, too. They find new ways to preserve food and make it taste better.

It is important to inspect our food to make sure
it is safe to eat. Meats and other foods are
checked for chemical pollution.

The government hires
chemists as food inspectors.
They make sure that the
chemicals that go into our
food are good. They keep
harmful chemicals out
of the foods we eat.

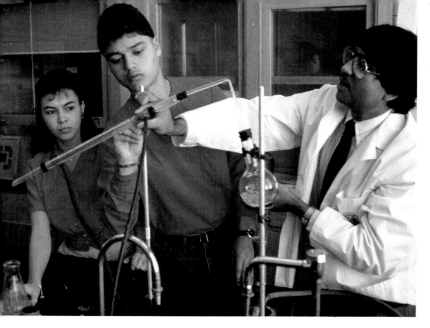

Chemistry is an important part of your school studies. Chemical experiments are often very exciting.

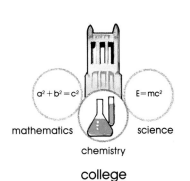

If you want to be a chemist, you must work hard. You must study all the mathematics and science you can. You must go to college. You must learn as much as you can.

What you learn in a chemistry class may help save our environment.

Who knows? Maybe someday your knowledge of chemistry may help solve some of the world's problems.

WORDS YOU SHOULD KNOW

acid rain(AS•uhd RAYN)—rainwater that has a high acid content

alloy(AL•oy)—a mixture of two or more different metals

atom(AT•uhm)—the smallest particle of matter

biochemist(by•oh•KEHM•ist)—a chemist who studies living things

calcium(KAL•see•uhm)—an element that living things need to form teeth and bones

chemical reaction(KEM•uh•kuhl ree•AK•shuhn)—an event in which atoms recombine with other atoms to form new materials

chemicals(KEM•uh•kuhlz)—materials that are used in fertilizers and in many manufacturing processes

chemistry(KEM•is•tree)—the science that studies what substances are made of, how they combine with other substances, and how they behave under certain conditions

compound(KAHM•pownd)—a material made from two or more elements joined together

decay(di•KAY)—to rot or break down

drug(DRUHG)—a substance that is used as a medicine

electricity(uh•lek•TRIS•uh•tee)—a form of energy that can produce heat and light

element(EL • uh • muhnt) — a material made of only one kind of atom

environment(en • VY • run • ment) — the things that surround us; the lands and waters of the Earth

food chain(FOOD CHAYN) — a relationship among organisms in which each feeds on a plant or on an animal below it in the chain and is then eaten by an animal above it

gas(GAS) — a substance that is not solid or liquid, but flows freely and is able to expand indefinitely

hydrogen(HY • druh • jen) — a very light element found in the form of a gas and mixed with oxygen in water

liquid(LIK • wid) — a substance that flows more or less freely and may be poured from its container

mercury(MER • kyu • ree) — a grayish white metal that is liquid at room temperature

oxygen(OX • uh • jen) — a gas that is found in the air and mixed with hydrogen in water

pharmacist(FAR • muh • sist) — a person who prepares medicines

poison(POY • zuhn) — a harmful substance that causes sickness or death if eaten or drunk

pollutants(puh • LOOT • uhnts) — materials that make the air or water unclean

solid(SAHL • uhd) — a substance that has a definite size and shape

tissue(TISH • yoo) — flesh; the muscles, bones, and organs of the body

PHOTO CREDITS

© Cameramann International, Ltd.—17, 20, 21 (right), 25

Dembinsky Photo Associates:
- © Stephen Graham—4 (top)
- © Larime Photographic—7 (insert), 22 (right)
- © John Mielcarek—9, 15 (both photos), 24 (left)
- © M. L. Dembinsky, Jr.—13 (right)
- © Sharon Cummings—16

Food and Drug Administration—26 (right)

InfoEdit:
- © Richard Hutchings—Cover

Photo Edit:
- © Michael Newman—21 (left), 23 (center)
- © Rhoda Sidney—4 (bottom left)
- © Robert Brenner—8, 23 (top left)
- © David Young-Wolff—10, 19 (bottom), 23 (right), 29
- © Anna E. Zuckerman—12
- © McCarten—19 (top left)
- © Alan Oddie—22 (left)
- © Tony Freeman—26 (left), 28 (right)
- © Paul Conklin—28 (left)

Root Resources:
- © Richard Jacobs—4 (bottom right)
- © Leonard Gordon—7
- © Don and Pat Valenti—13 (top left)

SIPA Press:
- © Alex—19 (top right)

Valan Photos:
- © Cancolosi—4 (center), 24 (right)
- © Phillip Norton—13 (center)
- © Gilbert Van Ryckevorsel—14 (both photos)

Courtesy of Walgreen Company—11

© Jim Whitmer—6, 27

Illustrations by Tom Dunnington

About the Author

Paul P. Sipiera is a professor of earth sciences at William Rainey Harper College in Palatine, Illinois. His principal research interests are in the study of meteorites and volcanic rocks. He has participated in the United States Antarctic Research Program and is a member of The Explorers Club. He is currently serving as president of the Planetary Studies Foundation. When he is not studying science, he can be found traveling the world or working on his farm in Galena, Illinois.